NIGHT RANGER

BY

MELVIN E BUNN

NIGHT RANGER

ISBN: 978-1-7341093-2-0 (PAPERBACK)
ISBN: 978-1-7341093-3-7 (EBOOK)

I want to dedicate this book to all the brave men and women who serve, who have served our country! Thank you for the service you rendered on our behalf. Words cannot express how much we appreciate all of you.

THIS PAGE INTENTIONALLY LEFT BLANK

CONTENTS

ACKNOWLEDGMENTS
INTRODUCTION
1. HOW IT BEGAN
2. THE REGULAR ARMY (RA)
3. RANGER COURSE
4. LIFE AFTER THE MILITARY
   SUMMARY

THIS PAGE INTENTIONALLY LEFT BLANK

ACKNOWLEDGMENTS

I want to thank my lovely wife of 30 years Mrs. Deborah for supporting me in all my endeavors. You have truly been a blessing to me! As I went from school to school and from state to state you helped me become a better leader and a better person. You have shown me what true compassion is and your love for your family is a testament to your character. To me, you are the best girl in the whole wide world.

I also want to thank each team leader, squad leader, platoon leader, and every leader that helped frame and develop me into being the man I am today. Thank you for not giving up on me but helping me to become all that I could be in the Army!

THIS PAGE INTENTIONALLY LEFT BLANK

INTRODUCTION

This book gives my personal experience as one of the first black Rangers from Lawton Oklahoma who went and completed Ranger training. I am going to highlight some of challenges I faced as a young black man.

I am going to share with you *how it began,* growing up in a small military town Ft. Sill/Lawton *AKA,* LA or the Lawton Area.

Then, I am going to discuss going from ROTC at Lawton High School to joining the Regular Army/ *RA*, as a combat engineer or a 12b. I did cohort training (*Basic/AIT*) at Ft. Lenard Wood, MO. I will talk about my first flight to Watertown, NY and my first duty station (*Ft. Drum*).

I will then share my experience how I signed up for Ranger school, went to Ranger school, my overall experience while in Ranger school.

The last thing I will talk about is the politics behind me leaving the military and my transition from the military life to the civilian life, my wife and my children.

The last thing I will do is summarize my story and get ready for the next chapter of my life.

(RIP) Relis Eugene Bunn
(1928-1971)

HOW IT BEGAN

When I was just a small lad, around 2 years old, my father passed away. He had just retired from the military around a year prior. He went to sleep and as my mother tells me the story, she was not able to wake him up so she called the ambulance which took him to the hospital which pronounced him dead upon arrival. She told me that the doctor told her that it looked as if he had a massive heart attack in his sleep.

The sting of death was not as hard on me as it was on my siblings because honestly, I was too young to remember him. So, I can only tell you what I heard, not necessarily what I know, about my father, but I have pieced the parts together. My mother said while we were at the grave site, I ask her if dad was going to wake up, she shook her head and told me "no, he is not". She said I was too young and I didn't understand what death was.

Since I was my father's dependent, the military took care of me until I reached the age of 18. You see, I have been a part of the military most of my life. Even though I was young, I still felt and still feel a void that only the loss of a parent can bring. I often wonder how life would have been if he was still alive. Sometimes I wish God would have granted him more time on this earth, but I am thankful for the life I have. My brother and sisters often speak of their love for him and how he was a good father which taught them life lessons and skill sets that they use and possess today.

I am told that my father was a financial genius that loved and provided for his family, even in his death he was teaching us life skills.

When he died, he left his family with a paid off house, a vehicle and enough liquidity and resources that we were able to make it and stay together as a family unit! He also had a life insurance policy which was a big help to us as well.

I do not know if he knew he was going to die but it seems like he was prepared!

Public Service Announcement (PSA)#1

A person never knows when their time is going to be up, so I believe one should prepare themselves by having an insurance policy that will help ease the financial responsibility of love ones that is left behind!

My mother remarried a young man named Willie James Truitt(deceased), I am so thankful for him that he stepped in and he guided us into manhood. He was a firm but a fair man, he encouraged us to be the best we could be. He loved us as if we were his own, he even wanted to adopt me and take his last name. I am glad that we had positive role models and I believe I turned out ok.

Growing up, I always knew I wanted to follow in my dad's footsteps.

I told my mother that I would one day join the military and travel the world like she did with my dad. Mom would often speak of how she and my dad would drive out to California to see and link up with his brother Bill. From my understanding, dad was close to his brothers and spent a lot of time with them. They also spent a lot of time up in the Chicago area with his brother my uncle Felix. He loved to travel and spent time with his siblings.

I was just a regular kid growing up, I played football and baseball for Mr. Wiley that lived down the street from us. I really enjoyed growing up in my neighborhood a small military community. My dad was originally from Hooks, Texas, a small one stop sign town, but the Lawton/Fort Sill community was offering black soldiers a couple of plots of land, which he purchased for pennies on the dollar and a shotgun house or a barrack. They just had to have the house moved from Fort Sill to their plot of land. Someone from Fort Sill saw the future and wanted to prepare the community for integration.

I still own that piece of property and it reminds me of where it all started for me, and in some since it causes me to think of my father and all the fond memories I had growing up in the house.

I often share with people why they may not recognize me from Lawton View, all my siblings went to Dunbar Elementary School (the only elementary school for blacks) but when it was my turn to go to the school, I was bused across town to a mixed school called Westwood Elementary. Westwood went from pre-k through 6th grade, and I never got the opportunity to go to an all-black school. They tell me that everyone knew one another and their parents, they say it was close knit, but I did not get a chance to experience it.

Society had begun to integrate kids into the melting pot. I was that first wave of black kids to be bused out of the neighborhood and across town. I often wonder how it would have been to have all black teachers, coaches and staff and police officers, but I guess it was for the best.

Through this experience I gained lifetime friends and a wealth of experiences that I will cherish for the rest of my time on this side of the dirt.

I met my lifetime friend Benjamin (Ben) Cross! Ben and I were like two peas in a pot. We did everything together including get into trouble, but that information is for another book.

We did not have a middle school we went directly to Junior High. I went to school at Tomlinson Junior High which I also was bused from my side of town. I was tall and lanky with a jerry curl. At Tomlinson, it seemed like I was always challenged as a young man to fight, it seemed to be a norm at Tomlinson to be picked on from the upperclassmen in our class. But I had a secret weapon, a person learned very quick that a young man had to be a good runner or a good fighter. I was neither one, but I had my friend Ben, and you could guarantee that if I had to fight my friend was right by my side fighting with me.

I will never forget how an upper classman right when the bell had rung walked by me and slapped all of my books out of my hand, little did he know that Ben was coming from the opposite direction and saw my books flying in the air. The next thing I know Ben had jumped up in the air and kicked the guy so hard that it knocked him down. We did not stand around to see it he was ok, but I did not have any more trouble out of him the rest of the year and I saw him just about every day.

Tomlinson was where I really learned the concept of teamwork. Sometimes in life you need people that will have your back and are willing to fight with you and for you.

Sometimes as boys growing up and developing into young men, we need structure and discipline, even if we have parents in the home. Sometimes it takes an outside voice to help guide and direct you in the right direction. For some reason kids tend to listen to other people besides their parents.

I finally graduated from Tomlinson Junior High School, it was on to Lawton High School, the home of the wolverines.

This would be the first school without my best friend and my security blanket. I did not know how I would do without him being there but, I was not that scrawny little kid anymore. I grew up just a tad bit, I was now 189 pounds and stood at 6 foot 2 inches tall. I could now fight, run and defend myself all on my own. I did not have to stay on the porch and just bark like I was going do something, but I had become the big Dogg!

I had a great time at Lawton High, there are so many memorable stories that I experienced while attending.

Most of my peers were interested in playing either football, baseball, or basketball.

I liked to have money in my pocket so during the summer break, I started working with one of my friends who was the manager of Lawton Janitorial Service (Kermit) So, I did not participate in sports at Lawton High. Kermit taught me how to be a good follower. He showed me the importance of listening to what was being said and the ability to follow the instructions that were given.

During my junior year at the high school, I joined ROTC. ROTC was so fun, I did not only learn the basic commands, drills, formations Etc., but I gained lifelong friends and comrades.

Since I knew what I wanted to do (join the military), I went to see the school's commander and talked to him, he recommended that I join the delayed entry program which would allow me to receive credit for ROTC before I went booth camp. I followed his advice and went in on the delayed entry program on November 21, 1986, when I went to boot camp, I went in as a PFC.

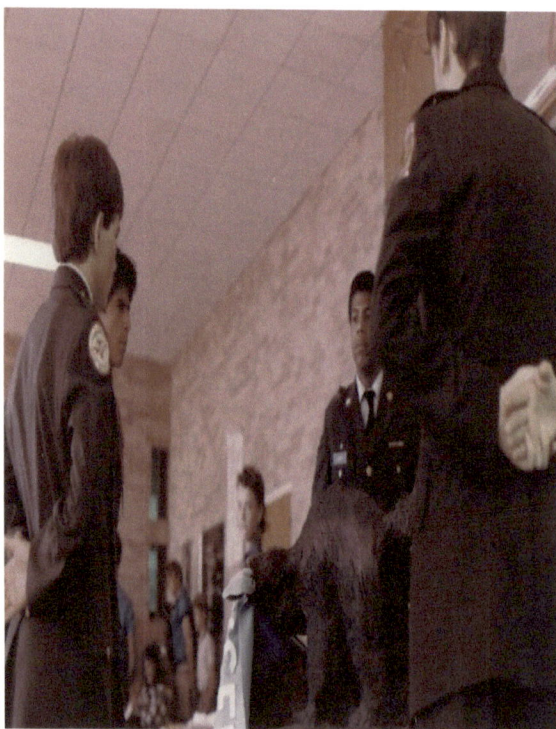

(Credits for Photo, LHS, yearbook committee 1986)

Military Training Certificate

RESERVE OFFICERS' TRAINING CORPS

This is to certify that MELVIN BERN

successfully completed 2 *years of instruction in the* JUNIOR

Reserve Officers' Training Corps, on 31 MAY , 19 85

given at LAWTON HIGH SCHOOL, LAWTON, OK

this 31st *day of* MAY *in the year of our Lord*

one thousand nine hundred and EIGHTY-SIX

Charles R Horton

CHARLES R HORTON
LTC, FA
SENIOR ARMY INSTRUCTOR

THIS PAGE INTENTIONALLY LEFT BLANK

THE REGULAR ARMY (RA)

I never will forget the day my recruiter came and picked me up from my house and drove me to Oklahoma City at the Military Entrance Processing Station (MEPS). It was not a bad winter that year, it had hardly snowed, but it was bitter cold. It was a couple of days after Christmas, December 30, 1986. I can still see the faces of the young men in a long line with me being processed into the service. Most of us had that look on our face like, what did I get myself into.

After making it through the medical line we had to get sworn in.

Ready or not, I was now an enlisted soldier in the United States Army.

UNITED STATES ARMY

CERTIFICATE OF ENLISTMENT

THIS IS TO CERTIFY THAT

MELVIN E. BUNN

HAS ENLISTED FOR SERVICE IN THE UNITED STATES ARMY

new member of the Army, you have demonstrated keen foresight by accepting the Army's
ge. You can be justly proud of your decision to enlist in the Army for service to your nati
e people of the United States are deeply grateful to you for your personal commitment
to national defense.

JAMES R. CAIN, JR.
LTC, MI
Commanding

21 NOV 86

DATE

We left directly from the MEP station to the Oklahoma City, bus station. I was on my way to Fort Leonard Wood, MO, as a Combat Engineer.

There were two other young men that went through the swearing in ceremony that were on their way to basic as well, but I did not know it at the time.

Like everyone else, I heard how basic training was and I was expecting the worst right off the get go. However, I arrived on a holiday weekend and the duty Sargent had to babysit a couple barracks full or new recruits.

He was so kind to us, all the horror stories I heard seem to be wrong, I thought. So, we spent the next couple of days getting ready for the drill instructors to come and get us.

It was a couple of recruits that really did not want to be there, I did not understand why a person would sign up and then want to quit. Later, that night I saw flashing lights at the other barracks and we found out later that morning a recruit tried to commit suicide by tying himself to a floor buffer and throwing it out the balcony of the second floor.

He was not successful because the cord was too long so, he just paid for a floor buffer; they sent him packing within that same hour.

The 1st fell on Sunday and we stayed in the barracks one more day.

Monday morning after we ate breakfast around 9am I heard a rumbling of what looked like cattle cars coming down the street. I cannot tell you how many there were but there were a lot of them.

The Sergeant in charge told us that our drill instructors would take good care of us for the next 8 weeks or so.

All of us had our bags in our hands, we begin to load the cattle cars, they packed us in like sardines. There was no room to sit, everyone had to stand. Everything seemed to be going ok until the cattle doors closed.

As soon as we started moving, the drill instructor told us to shut the F**k up, you could hear a pin drop it was so quit.

The ride took about 20 minutes, but it felt like an eternity.

The cattle cars finally stopped, and it seemed like in unison all the cattle doors came open all at once. The only thing you could hear is the drill instructors yelling and telling us to get the f**k off, I believe he threw a couple of guys with his hands because they were so slow.

I can never forget that first step off the cattle car, I heard yelling from every direction, recruits tripping over their bags, several in the leaning rest, I knew that I was not in Oklahoma anymore.

I would spend my entire basic and AIT training at Fort, Leonard Wood, I was in one of the first cohort units, the military was trying a new concept that keep the entire brigade from basic through AIT together.

DEPARTMENT OF THE ARMY

CERTIFICATE OF TRAINING

This is to certify that

PV2 MELVIN BUNK

has successfully completed

COMBAT ENGINEER TRAINING - MOS 12B10

B COMPANY, 583th BATTALION, 132D ENGINEER BRIGADE

Given at _____ FORT LEONARD WOOD, MO _____

JAMES V. BOYLE
CPT, EN
Commanding

Previous Edition Obsolete

After the completion of AIT, the brigade received orders to go to Fort. Drum, New York.

I had a layover a couple of days at my home in Lawton. I was getting ready to fly to Ft. Drum, New York. This was my first flight ever; I did not know what to expect. I was a little nervous and could not sleep the night before.

I got up early in the morning, I had to be at the airport about 6am for an 8 o'clock flight out.

I said goodbye to the group that came to the airport with me.

I walked down the terminal and glanced back and waved goodbye for the last time.

I get to my terminal and have a seat to wait for them to open the door so we could board the plane.

A lady in a uniform gets behind a microphone and welcome everyone to the flight and says they will be boarding soon.

She calls for first class first then the rest of us could board the plane.

The plane at the Lawton Airport was small and it sat around 25 people or so.

I was just a kid getting on the plane, I sat in the coach section in the middle of the plane.

The stewardess gets on it the intercom and goes through a safety check.

While she is going through the safety check, I hear the engine reave up.

It feels like we are being pushed back from the stairway we walked on to get inside the plane.

We begin to move toward a runway as the stewardess is finishing up the safety check.

The flight crew is locking down the drink carts and preparing for takeoff.

After the safety briefings, the captain come over the intercom and welcome us to the flight.

He says that it should be smooth flighting until we reached our destination, the first leg was to Dallas Fort Worth International Airport. I will never forget the sun beaming through the window, it looked clean and calm.

We got to the end of the runway and the captain puts the fasten seat belt sign on. He comes back on the intercom and tell us that the tower has given us permission to take off and we would be in the air shortly.

It seemed like as soon as he turned off the intercom, it begins to roll forward.

The plane stops and turns in the direction that we are going to take off.

It was the first leg of my journey, riding on it felt like driving fast in an old truck on a holey road.

I made it to Dallas Fort Worth International Airport, I had to run to get to the right terminal which was on the other side of the airport.

Once again, we boarded the plane, this time I am boarding a 747 that had 366 seats and I sat over the wing on that plane. The first 16 seats were first class, the Airlines sat them first.

When everyone got settled, the stewardess came by and checked the tickets.

I was so nervous I really could not relax that well.

The stewardess gets on it the intercom and goes through a safety check.

The flight crew is locking down the drink carts and preparing for takeoff.

After the safety briefings, the captain comes over the intercom and welcome us to the flight.

He tells us that the sun may be shinning in Dallas, but it is snowing in New York. He says that we are going to ascend to thirty thousand feet in the air and the flight will take about an hour fifteen minutes.

We got to the end of the runway and the captain puts the fasten seat belt sign on. He comes back on the intercom and tell us that the tower has given us permission to take off and we would be in the air shortly.

I hear the engine beginning to roar, it feels like he is holding the brakes at the same time. The hair on the back of my head is beginning to stand up. With a quick thrust my body is propelled backwards in the seat as the plane begins to move forward swiftly down the runway. It feels one fast rollercoaster ride. The next thing I know the noise of the plane goes up in the air about 45 degrees' in the air and the ground begins to move away as I hear the wheel folding in under the belly of the plane.

My ears are popping currently, I just so happen to have a piece of bubble gum in my pocket. I take it out and start chewing on it.

We make it to 30,000 feet in no time, the seat belt sign comes off. The stewardess starts serving drinks, peanuts and cookies.

A person could tell that the flight crew worked like a well-oiled machine.

Just as quick as we made it to cruising altitude the captain put the seat belt sign on. He tells the stewardess to prepare the cabin for descent.

We begin coming down from 30,000 feet through the clouds. The sun was shining above the clouds but as soon as we went through the clouds, it became dark and it started raining and the lower we descended it begin to snow big pretty flakes falling from the sky.

I must have looked nervous because the flight attendant came and stood right beside me and talked to me for a minute or so, she reassured me that everything would be ok.

We landed at John F. Kennedy International Airport, and getting off the plane, I knew I was not in Oklahoma anymore. Maybe it is just their culture, but the average New Yorker carries a somewhat serious demeaner. They look like it is all about business.

I had to go and get my bags from the baggage area. I did not have that much but I was glad that it made it with me.

I went to the information counter and inquired about getting to Ft. Drum, the lady at the desk told me that the only way to get to Ft. Drum was to either take a small plane up to Watertown or see it a cap driver was going to be driving up that direction.

By chance, I was standing there when a couple more of my cohort team came to inquire about getting to Ft. Drum.

A cab driver with his Hussle overheard the helpdesk conversation and rushed over and suggested he could drive us up to Watertown for 50 dollars apiece. There were 3 of us at that time and we all agreed that that would be our best option since the next flight was not guaranteed since it was snowing, most of the flights had begun to be canceled.

The ride was going to take about 45 minutes so we loaded the minivan and off we went. The traffic was crazy until we made it to the outskirts of the city.

The cab driver was not playing around, he was driving that cab like he stole it or something.

We finally made it to Watertown, New York, it was a small town with not much to see, it took all of 10 minutes to get from one side of town to the other.

A short time later I see a big sign that says, welcome to Fort Drum Light Infantry Division.

THIS PAGE INTENTIONALLY LEFT BLANK

Fort Drum Light Infantry Division

The cab driver drops us off at the headquarters buildings of the combat engineers.

We exit the cab, and we are greeted by a duty Sergeant which looks at our orders and send us to our different companies.

For the next year, I spent most of my time in the field, our unit conducted a lot of training as a combat engineer.

One of the first people that I saw was our first Sergeant Smith, he was a bad man, he was an Airborne Ranger, a Seal. He was on his way out of the service, but he was my inspiration to do great things.

Since we were a light infantry unit, most of my equipment was on my back. We carried over 150 pounds in our ruck sacks.

Our unit had all the updated equipment including but not limited to the hummer AKA humv, M16A2.

We did a lot of training that year, I could only think is, "wow is this what being a combat engineer is all about".

Our main task was to be ready to deploy within 18 of being called on and we trained like we were being deployed at any time.

Fort Drum stayed about 70 degrees in the summertime and in the wintertime, it was bitter cold, colder than what I was used too; there was a lot of lake effect snow and it was cold.

I remember the nights being cold and the stars being bright.

At Fort Drum, I was in fairly good shape, for my PT test I ran 2 miles in 11 minutes and 36 seconds. We also did a 100 sit ups and 100 push-ups.

I had a regiment of working out after the last formation. My work out days consisted of running to the gym which was about 2 miles away and swimming laps in the pool. After doing laps in the pool, I would get dressed and run back to the barracks.

I would run up the street to the late cafeteria to get a night snack.

My first official course I went to was called the light fighters' course, I was a PV2, just green.

This course started me on a path that would somewhat define my military career. Most of the instructors were infantry sergeants who had some experience fighting in some type of conflict.

10th MOUNTAIN DIVISION (LIGHT INFANTRY)

THIS IS TO CERTIFY THAT

CLIMB TO GLORY

MOUNTAIN

PVT MELVIN E. BUNN,

HAS RISEN TO THE CHALLENGE AND SUCCESSFULLY COMPLETED
THE LIGHT FIGHTERS COURSE PHASE 1
40 HOURS

LTC, IN
Commanding

GIVEN THIS _22nd_ DAY OF _May 1987_

LOCATED AT _Ft Drum, NY_

FORM

MOUNTAIN

41st
ENGINEER BATTALION

CERTIFICATE OF ACHIEVEMENT

AWARDED TO

PFC MELVIN E. BUNN

For Successful Completion of

LIGHT FIGHTERS
Phase II
SAPPERS FORWARD

80 HOURS

VIGOR ET VALOR

Unlike the average solider, I volunteered for every little class or course that came available. It was not many classes that I turned down; I cannot think of one.

I was promoted to PFC and went to Light Fighters'2 course in November of 1987.

Going to classes kept me away from being in one place for too long. It also gave me a comfort level in working with people or other soldiers I did not know.

I was just going to different courses and one day a new Sergeant came to our company I cannot remember his name, but he acted like no one was good enough unless they had a Ranger tab or had been to Ranger school.

He had been to Ranger school and failed and he was trying to make it back, but his knees were bad.

Jim Crowley was in my squad a team member; Jim was talking almost trash to the new Sergeant as to say he could pass the physical part of Ranger school. You can imagine how that conversation went since Jim was from Boston with that heavy eastern slang.

I just laughed but Jim was right, the 10th mountain division kept us in tip top condition.

In those days, in order to go to Ranger school or be considered eligible to try out for the school, you would have to attend a combat leaders' course.

The division tried to weed out the soldiers that they thought would not qualify for the school. They attempted to mimic the Ranger school PT and some of the mental aspects of the course.

Jim raised his hand and said that he wanted to attend the course so he would be eligible to go to Ranger school.

He went to the combat leadership training and passed the course; Jim came back to the unit talking more trash.

I do not know if it were my competitive nature or what, but I said to myself, if Jim could go and pass it, so could I.

The next day I asked the sergeant could I attend the leadership training, he asked me if I intended to go to Ranger school.

Of course, I told him yes, but I really did not have any intention in going to Ranger school. If I would have said no, there he probably would have gave the slot to another solider that wanted to go to Ranger school. There were several soldiers that wanted to become a Ranger, we were light infantry division, we did not know any better, it was in our nature.

So, if it had not been for Jim, I probably would have never gone to Ranger school.

Then 2 spots came open for ranger school, Jim and another soldier from one of the other units got their chance to go, Jim was on his way to Ranger school and I was on my way to the combat leaders' course.

Combat leaders' course was a 10-day course that really focused on some areas that the average soldier did not work on. For example, we were forced to swim a pools length in full gear.

The course itself was not that hard mainly PT and the instructors played a lot of mind tricks. They kept us up 2 or 3 days out of the 10. They pushed our mind and body to see if they could break us.

I was strong willed and strong as an ox; I knew how to play the game even if I did not say anything. I was like a sponge that took everything in but acted like I was crazy so I would not get any unwanted attention.

There were soldiers from all over the base from different MOS's, but mainly 11b's, there was even a female soldier in the combat leaders' course that was bad to the bone, she was proving a point that she was physically strong enough to compete with the rest of us. She wanted to be the first female to go to Ranger school in the 10th mountain division, I believed her. We graduated from the course in July of 1988.

As I finished the course Jim had left for Ranger School. My intentions were to wait for Jim to come back from Ranger school and share with me what it took to make it through the course.

Jim left at the end of July, so that meant he should not have come back until October. The next thing I knew Jim had made it back to Fort Drum.

His body language and his demeaner told the entire story, so I never had that conversation with Jim about Ranger school.

I kind of got cold feet and put Ranger school on hold for a minute, I had figured if Jim could not pass it, I did not think I could pass it, his failure caused me to lose confident in my own abilities.

I finally got the opportunity to go to Ranger school about a year later, one day the word came down that they needed someone that had been to the combat leaders' course to take a slot that was available for our unit.

Of course, since I had been to the course and successfully passed it, I was top of the pecking list.

I cannot remember the exact month I left going to Fort Benning, but it was after my birthday which is in August so a good guess would be mid-September or the first part of October.

I can tell you that when I got there it was so hot that sweat would soak your BDU's just by standing outside for a couple of minutes. When I left Fort Benning for the last time, there was snow on the ground, and I did not think that Georgia received that much snow.

44

DEPARTMENT OF THE ARMY

CERTIFICATE OF TRAINING

This is to certify that

PFC MELVIN E. BUNN,

has successfully completed

Combat Leaders Course 8-88

11 - 22 JULY 1988 (160 HRS)

Given at FORT DRUM, N.Y. 13602-5000

HERBERT J. LLOYD

THIS PAGE INTENTIONALLY LEFT BLANK

THIS PAGE INTENTIONALLY LEFT BLANK

RANGER COURSE

Ranger school is one of the most challenging military schools in the world, the last time I researched only 49% of the soldiers that attempted the course have succeeded.

The main problem is that the average soldier cannot reach the general technical score AKA the GT score of 105 or higher which includes a fitness test (58 push-ups, 69 sit-ups, a five-mile run in less than 40 minutes or less and 6 pull-ups), Completion of a water assessment test, a 12-mile march with a 35-pound rucksack and a weapon in less than 3 hours.

The average soldier did not come from a light infantry company or a ranger battalion. They were not used to putting that amount of stress on their body in such a short amount of time.

Being in shape is half the battle for most of the courses I went through while I was in the military. The other part was the mental games and warfare they would play on your mind to try to get you to quit.

The first thing I saw when I reached the compound of the Ranger school was a big bolder/rock that was about 6-foot-tall and about 4 feet wide. The closer I got to the rock; I see that it was boot prints facing downward like a soldier was in the leaning rest.

I chuckled because I knew exactly what they were saying by using the rock to illustrate that a person had to have a rock mentality to go through this course.

From the time we entered the complex until the time we finished the course was everything that rock promised pure mental and physical stress on a body that they could throw on you.

The year I went to Ranger school they had 4 phases, the land phase, the mountain phase, the water phase and the desert phase.

THIS PAGE INTENTIONALLY LEFT BLANK

Phase 1

The first phase set the tone for the rest of the phases. Every morning we started out by hitting the ground running, it seemed like endless trails and routes that a different instructor would lead the way every morning. It was before the sun came up, the fresh smell of the cutting morning dew in the air. The first morning and all the time at Phase 1, during PT, a 5 ton or what we called a duce, and a half would be following the companies of soldiers. From the first moment you arrived on the base, they encouraged you to quit and they were not playing any games. As soon as a candidate said they quit, they were sent to the headquarters and cut orders to go back to their unit. That began before we did PT every morning and it really did not matter when you quit it seemed like that truck was following us around everywhere, we went.

We probably lost about 20 soldiers before the end of PT, that 5 ton was full of dejected soldiers. It seemed like it took less than 30 minutes, and they were processed out and leaving the Ranger compound.

When we finished PT, it seemed like we did not have a lot of time to get dressed but we changed into our BDU's and went to our first training class of the day, before breakfast.

At some point in time, we lined up to go to breakfast but before we were able to eat, we had to do 6 pull-ups before you could eat. In front on the chow hall were 4 individual set of pull up bars were located. Each of the pull-up bars was the same height. It was designed so that a soldier would have to run and jump upward and then hang in a Deadman's position before they had to do 6 pull-ups from a hanging stop. If a soldier was not able to do the 6 pull-ups, they were doing push-ups until everyone else ate and then they sent you to the end of the line and had to inhale their food down because they failed that task.

It sounds quite simple, but those pull-up bars had to be at least 7 feet tall or so. I stood at 6'3 and I had to get a good leap in order to reach the bar. Unfortunately, we lost another 20 soldiers or so during breakfast time at the pull-up bars.

I was fortunate to be in great shape. I adjusted to this routine very quick, after each meal we went directly back to another training session. A little more PT between each class we would run from the one to the other class, this was all before lunch break.

The lunch break followed the same process, we had to line up outside the chow hall, run up to the pull-up bars and do our 6 pull-ups and then get in line to enter the chow hall.

The same pull-up bar, they did not get lower and the soldiers that were weak at breakfast time either tried harder to do the 6 pull-ups or quit on the spot.

The instructors would antagonize the soldiers telling us 'remember, you'll volunteered for this school, you can quit anytime you get ready' they just wanted you to come see them.

The first two weeks it seemed like people were falling like flies, here today and gone today.

The rest of the group ate and got back in formation so we could proceed on to the next training assignment. Our first day ended with some advanced combat training techniques. That training gave us some much-needed stress relief.

Our dinner meal followed the same process, the pull-up bars, and the dinner. They must have felt sorry for us or something, maybe it was the fact that so many had quit and dropped out so early, but whatever it was, we were able to see the sun set.

Maybe they thought they had pushed us to hard and wanted to give us a break but whatever it was I sure was glad that day.

I want to say that Phase one repeated itself day after day until the last day. People were still dropping out of the course but less and less each day.

By mid-week, I started to feel my BDU's getting a little looser and my face begin to get thinner because they had us exercising more than the calories, we were consuming so our body begin to eat the fat.

The last day would take its toll on every soldier that wasn't used to carrying a rucksack with weight inside of it. The instructors took us on a force march. I did not know and did not care how long it was, I was just ready for it to end.

This was one of the last obstacles they used in Phase one for the weeding out process.

That 5 ton was full of bodies that day, the rest of us continued with training while the dejected soldiers begin to process out of the compound.

THIS PAGE INTENTIONALLY LEFT BLANK

Phase 2

Phase two was the mountain phase. We got up early in the morning before the sun came up, there were buses waiting on us to load. It took about 3 hours or so to get there.

Along the way, one of the instructors that was following us to the camp site accidently ran off the side on a cliff in his jeep.

So, the entire convoy stopped and rendered aid to him, we never heard if he was ok because the training continued.

We finally reached our destination we were late for breakfast because of the accident so we were properly introduced to our new set of instructors by going directly to the firing range.

Although in Phase 2 we did not do a lot of PT it was still a very physically demanding phase.

I remember doing some weapons training, knot training, repelling, forced marches just to name a few.

There were a different set of instructors every Phase even though the main set handled the day-to-day activities.

This Phase is where we started to get more hands-on training, this Phase was the start of individual evaluations by the instructors.

During this Phase is when is started to get a little colder. The stars really were big and bright at night. It seemed like the brighter they became the colder it got.

I will never forget this Phase because of the repelling training. I loved most of the training in this Phase, it is what we did at Drum all the time, I.E rock climbing, repelling, knot tying.

One incident that had me laughing. We were getting ready to repel and the instructor decided to make it a buddy repel instead of an individual repel. I guess they thought it would be funny to team me up with a little guy he had to have been no taller than 5'3 or shorter. I was thinking to myself; this was going to be easy but when it was our turn to repel, the instructors hooked me to the back of the little fellow.

Now I am not normally a fearful person, but it was training so I was not going to say no to them. I was about 190 pounds or so and the other soldier looked like he weighed 100 pounds soaking wet.

The side of the mountain we were repelling down was a sharp drop about 10 feet then another 50 to 60 feet before you reached the ground.

I hooked up to the little fellow and now it was all up to him to first lean back over the mountains edge in the L position.

Reaching this position by yourself is easy but with an extra 190 pounds on your back, I felt sorry for him. My fears were justified because he struggled carrying this big fellow and as soon as he started leaning back his knees gave way and we went vertical; I was so thankful that day because the belay was ready to save us. It scared every bodily fluid out of me that day but I guess that is why they emphasized safety at the beginning of each Phase.

As we reached the bottom of the mountain, he was too nervous to continue, I did not see him anymore during that Phase, I cannot remember if he passed that Phase or not.

After a long week of training, we finally had a chance to catch our breath. The instructors promised us a treat the next morning.

Most of us thought that was a code for applying more pressure to us but to our surprise, as we lined up for breakfast and went inside to eat the breakfast there it was.

The instructors told us that our group came at the right time of the year, it was blueberry season and we were treated with blueberry pancakes. I do not know if my body was just deprived of sugar or what but those were some of the best pancakes I ever ate.

I had gone to heaven for the short time I was inside eating my pancakes. Nothing could bother me the rest of the time I was in Phase 2. They could have thrown me off a bridge, I did not care because I was full and happy at that point. Sometimes it is just the small things in life that a person needs to help them to the next level.

Public Service Announcement (PSA)#2

You cannot look at a person and know what they are going through. It is important to listen to people when they talk, you may be the one person that can lead them to help. If you are a Veteran considering suicide please call the suicide prevention hotline 1(800)273-8255 and press 1, it is a free, anonymous, confidential resource that is available to anyone, even if you are not registered with the VA!

Unfortunately, Ranger school was the first time but not the last time I experienced losing a fellow Soldier. Although it been over 30 years it is still embedded in my brain that can be replayed by a sound or smell and sometimes a movie.

We were conducting a live fire mission (Raid), the entire class were divided into our different groups. One group conducted the main mission while another group provided security and watch and the last group provided cover and concealment.

For that mission, the team I was on provided illumination and cover for our team on the ground.

It was staged during the day and took place at night. It was supposed to be a simple mission, in and out but this time it was not.

As in each Phase they conducted a safety briefing telling us what would happen and the different scenario's we needed to be aware of.

As the live fire exercise was being conducted, one of the soldiers was hit by a bullet. The range went cold while he was medevacked out but he did not make it.

We were reminded that the training that we were conducting mimicked real life.

Phase 2 was over and as in Phase 1 the rest of the soldiers that made the cut got on the buses and we went back down the mountain and headed towards Florida for Phase 3.

THIS PAGE INTENTIONALLY LEFT BLANK

Phase 3

Phase 3 was the water phase and as expected, it lived up to its name. If you are familiar with Florida, one thing you can count on is the rain. It usually rains at least 2 times a day and then the humidity is a killer.

We did not get that many hot meals while there, mainly MRE's.

I cannot remember one, maybe it was because I was cold and wet, very miserable most of the time.

As soon as we were handed off to our new instructors, we hit the ground running. We went to our first training site right off the buses.

I never will forget that first day, the wind was high, and we were overlooking what appeared to be a small river that was rising due to the rain and it was moving fast.

Both banks had trees on both sides and looking across I could see people on the other side looking toward us.

What was supposed to happen is the instructors were supposed to be demonstrating how to successfully swim across the river with rope and tie it off using the knot methods you learned in Phase 2 to a tree so the other team members could cross over to the other side hooked into the rope.

What happened was, the current was so swift and strong that when the instructor went to swim to the other side the current begins to pull him down stream. Eventually, he became too weak to fight against the current and it begin to pull him under.

Even though he had his Ranger tab and was an instructor did save him that day, it was the team of instructors around him that saves his life that day.

In each Phase they took safety serious first before anything else including training, so before he went in the water, they put a rescue boat downstream just in case something happened. As we looked on, they jumped into action to save their comrade.

We moved on to the next mission, we ended up coming back to complete this training later in the week when the river was a little calmer.

The main thing I believe they wanted us to learn is the ability to perform missions on a boat and in the water while navigating in wet and a little or no sleep condition.

All the missions were basic infantry missions with different water elements and water equipment.

Our boots stayed submerged in water doing this entire phase. At the end of this Phase my feet looked like they had been beat with a meat cleaver and dry rioted.

I was so happy to finish Phase 3 and go on to the last Phase.

Before we went to Phase 4, we had a Christmas Break for a week or so. One of the hardest things was to leave that camp and report back in that short amount of time, but that is exactly what we did. I just spent time in Georgia until I had to report back, I was afraid if I went back to Fort Drum, I probably would not have gone back to Ranger school.

THIS PAGE INTENTIONALLY LEFT BLANK

Phase 4

Phase 4 was in Utah, this was supposed to be our desert, training. It was so cold out there that the time kind of dragged on and on. I was just ready to go but I had to play the game. The days were short, and the nights were long. Speaking of nights, I remember Utah having some big rabbits that glowed in the dark. I cannot recall the base name that we were on, but I believe it was the Nuclear test site because at night we could hear those rockets fire up and besides, it was a big sigh surrounded by an electrical fence with Nuclear signs all around the fence. I believe it was Dugway proving ground.

This is a Phase I will never forget either because this was the Phase I was recycled at.

After completing all the missions, we had to complete an evaluation form. The instructors asked us to fill out the form and rate our teammates. One of our teammates suggested that we rate each other so none of us would fail. The instructor came back and told us that someone had to fail and that if we did not fail someone, everyone would be recycled, he said it was up to us.

This was my first time in Ranger school and in the military that I was introduced to politics. I was used to getting a pass or fail on my own merit, not a group decision.

I knew how it was going to end, I was better than over half the group I was on, no if, ands, or buts about it however; I was the only Combat Engineer in the group.

Most of those guys were Infantry soldiers and no way were they going to allow me to pass and one of them be recycled.

I was ready to go home but most of the guys in my group was married and some had kids, so I did not really mind but could not stand the politics.

I lost a level of respect for the instructors because they were more concerned about keeping their fail rate numbers high.

I was recycled, I had to wait a day or so until the next class came along, it was just a couple of days.

I finally finished up and made it to graduation.

67

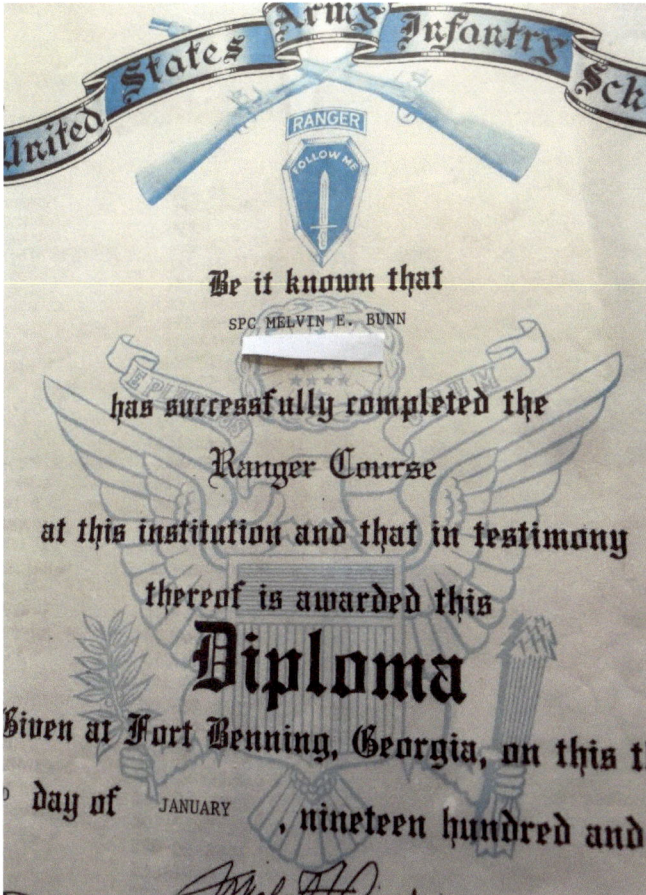

THIS PAGE INTENTIONALLY LEFT BLANK

RANGER

RECOGNIZING THAT I VOLUNTEERED AS A RANGER, FULLY KNOWING THE HAZARDS OF MY CHOSEN PROFESSION, I WILL ALWAYS ENDEAVOR TO UPHOLD THE PRESTIGE, HONOR, AND HIGH SPIRIT-DE-CORPS OF MY RANGER REGIMENT.

ACKNOWLEDGING THE FACT THAT A RANGER IS A MORE ELITE SOLDIER WHO ARRIVES AT THE CUTTING EDGE OF BATTLE BY LAND, SEA, OR AIR. I ACCEPT THE FACT THAT AS A RANGER MY COUNTRY EXPECTS ME TO MOVE FURTHER, FASTER, AND FIGHT HARDER THAN ANY OTHER SOLDIER.

NEVER SHALL I FAIL MY COMRADES, I WILL ALWAYS KEEP MYSELF MENTALLY ALERT, PHYSICALLY STRONG, AND MORALLY STRAIGHT AND I WILL SHOULDER MORE THAN MY SHARE OF THE TASK, WHATEVER IT MAY BE, ONE HUNDRED PERCENT AND THEN SOME.

GALLANTLY WILL I SHOW THE WORLD THAT I AM A SPECIALLY SELECTED AND WELL-TRAINED SOLDIER. MY COURTESY TO SUPERIOR OFFICERS, NEATNESS OF DRESS, AND CARE OF EQUIPMENT SHALL SET THE EXAMPLE FOR OTHERS TO FOLLOW.

ENERGETICALLY WILL I MEET THE ENEMIES OF MY COUNTRY. I SHALL DEFEAT THEM ON THE FIELD OF BATTLE FOR I AM BETTER TRAINED AND WILL FIGHT WITH ALL MY MIGHT. SURRENDER IS NOT A RANGER WORD. I WILL NEVER LEAVE A FALLEN COMRADE TO FALL INTO THE HANDS OF THE ENEMY AND UNDER NO CIRCUMSTANCES WILL I EVER EMBARRASS MY COUNTRY.

READILY WILL I DISPLAY THE INTESTINAL FORTITUDE REQUIRED TO FIGHT ON TO THE RANGER OBJECTIVE AND COMPLETE THE MISSION, THOUGH I BE THE LONE SURVIVOR.

RANGERS LEAD THE WAY!

70

Assistant Division Commander
10th Mountain Division (Light Infantry)
Fort Drum, New York 13602-5000

February , 1990

SPC Melvin Bunn
41st Engineer Battalion
Fort Drum, New York 13602

Dear Specialist Bunn,

Congratulations on your graduation from Ranger School! You have accomplished a feat that very few soldiers achieve---successful completion of the Army's toughest school. The Division is very proud of you.

Now we need you to employ all that you have learned to help make the 10th Mountain Division (Light Infantry) the best division in the Army. Our soldiers deserve the benefit of your newly-acquired skills.

Again, congratulations. You did a great job

Climb to Glory,

John D. Howard
Brigadier General, U.S. A
Assistant Division Commar

THIS PAGE INTENTIONALLY LEFT BLANK

I made it back to Fort Drum, I was excited but tired from being gone for so long. I had about a month rest and started going back to school. That year 1990, was a busy year, I was lateralled to the rank of corporal in January. I started going back to school in April, I went to primary leadership development course (PLDC) on the 12th and field sanitation training on the 23rd.

I was promoted to the rank of Sergeant on May 1st! I was so proud of myself for pushing myself and being able to complete the courses that an average soldier would not be able to accomplish.

Many of the soldiers that went to basic and AIT training with me seem to be proud to know that one of their own had accomplished such a great task.

I did not act arrogant or walk around with my chest stuck out but it felt like I had to always walk on eggshells. Especially around the old sergeants and corporal that were stuck in the same place since we got there.

I believe that a good leader was supposed to take soldiers under their wing and make them better with the information they gave them.

When I came back from Ranger school, I was not really given any guidance it was almost like they were telling me or showing me that they were going to keep all the information and experience they had to themselves.

For me it was either sink or swim and for the most part I did ok but I could have done better if I had a mentor.

I sure did miss first Sergeant Smith; he would understand how I felt and he would have been glad to be my mentor.

I believe a mentor is someone who has been where you are going and willing to help you get there.

At this part of my career, most of the people that were considered my peers were jealous of me because it took them years to get where I was, I took what a person would call a fast track.

I made E-5 in a little over 3 years of coming into the service. And for most of the sergeants that had been in 10 years plus and was still an E-5, I was on my way to becoming an E-5p, I was surprisingly good at boards.

It might have been me but everything I did was not good enough for them, the older

sergeants seem to try to sabotage anything I did
or wanted to do with the squads I was with.

For example, I went to jungle operation
training at Fort Sherman, Panama in June the 2-
22.

I remember one time, our platoon sergeant was
Sergeant Jefferson, I believe he was an E-8
waiting for a company to be a first Sergeant, I
do not know if he ever saw his self in the mirror
but he was a mean cuss. I was usually a happy
go lucky kind of guy but could turn on the dime
if I were pushed the wrong way. He walked
around with his chest stuck out and nothing a
person did could please him. He acted like an
old timer but he was not that old. I was a team
leader at the time and we got into it because he
told me to do something and then wanted to
micromanage the process that I was using. I
was tired of him that day; I was not going to
have no part of what he was doing and saying to
me that day. Just by chance it was a new
sergeant named Sgt Martinez that had just
moved to Fort Drum and deployed with us saw
how he was treating me and stood up for me.
Sergeant Jefferson was hot that he stepped in

and took my side. I am glad he did because I had planned on taking my equipment off and fighting right then and there. That probably would have been a good fight but we never got that chance. I am thankful to Sgt Martinez for stepping in when he did.

When we made it back to Fort Drum and since Sgt Jefferson could not control me or help me to develop, he decided to suck up to the New LT that had just came into our company and had me moved to another company. That probably was a good move because I had lost all respect for him as a leader.

Public Service Announcement (PSA)#3

Leaders are not born they are developed, remember treat people how they want to be treated because you may not treat yourself that well. I call it the golden rule, no matter your position your status quo it is good to respect one another and it does not hurt to be kind. We may disagree or even hold different political views but we can agree to disagree.

I got married on July 1st, 1990 at Sweet Heaven Holy Church of God by the honorable bishop Nathaniel C. Johnson.

I went on vacation for 2 weeks it was my honeymoon and I took my time and drove my wife from Fort Drum to Hampton Virginia where she was going to school.

I made it back to Fort Drum and 2 weeks later August 2, 1990, we went to war, Desert Storm desert shield. Our unit like everyone else's unit was on high alert. The war moved so quick that it was over with before it really got started.

I was enjoying life, living it to the fullest. I was like a big sponge absorbing everything I could.

When I came back from Ranger school, I asked my company commander (CO) would it be possible to go to Airborne Course, he was a believer in allowing his men to go anywhere it benefited them to advance their career and it made him look good when he could count on us to complete the task. Just like Ranger school, it was a list but most of the slots were given to infantry soldiers but my CO pushed for me to go because I had passed Ranger School. Most of the slots stayed full but one came open and I took the slot and completed the airborne course on the 7th of December 1990.

It was official, I was a 12b with P/V identifiers or a Combat Engineer/Airborne Ranger.

THIS PAGE INTENTIONALLY LEFT BLANK

DEPARTMENT OF THE ARMY

THIS IS TO CERTIFY THAT THE SECRETARY OF THE ARMY HAS AWARDED

THE ARMY ACHIEVEMENT MEDAL

SERGEANT MELVIN E. BUNN
HEADQUARTERS COMPANY, 41ST ENGINEER BATTALION

TO

FOR EXCEPTIONAL MERITORIOUS SERVICE FROM 1 APRIL 1987 TO DECEMBER 1991 WHILE ASSIGNED
TO THE 41ST ENGINEER BATTALION. DURING THIS PERIOD, SERGEANT BUNN DISPLAYED
OUTSTANDING EXPERTISE, INITIATIVE, PROFESSIONALISM AND DEDICATION TO DUTY. HIS
SELF DISCIPLINE AND MOTIVATION WERE EXEMPLIFIED BY HIS SUCCESSFUL COMPLETION OF
SEVERAL SCHOOLS, TO INCLUDE RANGER AND AIRBORNE. HE HAS PERFORMED EXCEPTIONALLY
AS BOTH A TEAM LEADER AND A TRAINING NCO ON SEVERAL DEPLOYMENTS AND FIELD
EXERCISES. SERGEANT BUNN'S OUTSTANDING PERFORMANCE TO DUTY REFLECTS GREAT CREDIT
UPON HIM, THE 10TH MOUNTAIN DIVISION AND THE UNITED STATES ARMY.

FROM: 1 APRIL 1987 TO 28 DECEMBER 1991.

GIVEN UNDER MY HAND IN THE CITY OF WASHINGTON
THIS 20th DAY OF December 19 91

JAMES L. HICKEY
LTC, EN
Commanding
ORDERS # 70-001

SECRETARY OF THE ARMY

DEPARTMENT OF THE ARMY

THIS IS TO CERTIFY THAT THE UNITED STATES ARMY HAS AWARDED

THE GOOD CONDUCT MEDAL

TO

SPECIALIST MELVIN E. BUNN

FOR EXEMPLARY BEHAVIOR, EFFICIENCY AND FIDELITY

IN ACTIVE FEDERAL MILITARY SERVICE

FROM 30 DECEMBER 1986 TO 29 DECEMBER 1989

81

United States Military Academy
West Point, New York

CERTIFICATE OF APPRECIATION
IS PRESENTED TO

SGT Melvin E. Bunn

FOR OUTSTANDING WORK IN SUPPORT OF CADET FIELD
TRAINING 1991 FROM 25 JUNE TO 14 AUGUST 1991.
YOUR PROFESSIONALISM AND DEDICATION TO DUTY
CONTRIBUTED TO THE OVERALL SUCCESS OF THE
MOBILITY/COUNTERMOBILITY/SURVIVABILITY
COMMITTEE. IN EVERY ENDEAVOR, YOU SURPASSED THE
ENGINEER MOTTO, "ESSAYONS." PROVIDED EXPERT
INSTRUCTION AND CHALLENGING TRAINING FOR THE
USMA CLASSES OF '92, '93 AND '94. YOUR
INDIVIDUAL AND COLLECTIVE EFFORTS ESTABLISHED A
MODEL FOR THE CADET CADRE IN "HOW TO TRAIN."

BARRY TOTTEN
LTC, EN
Chief, M/C/S Committee

UNITED STATES ARMY FORT BRAGG

XVIII ABN CORPS

Noncommissioned Officer Academy

BASIC
NONCOMMISSIONED OFFICER COURSE

Diploma

SERGEANT MELVIN E. BUNN

has successfully completed BNCOC class 1-92

program of instruction at this academy from 27 Oct through 06 Dec 19 91

GARY E. HOCK
Commander

Commandant

BONUS DUX BONUM REDDIT MILITEM

DUTY   DIGNITY   PATRIOTISM   RESPECT

THIS PAGE INTENTIONALLY LEFT BLANK

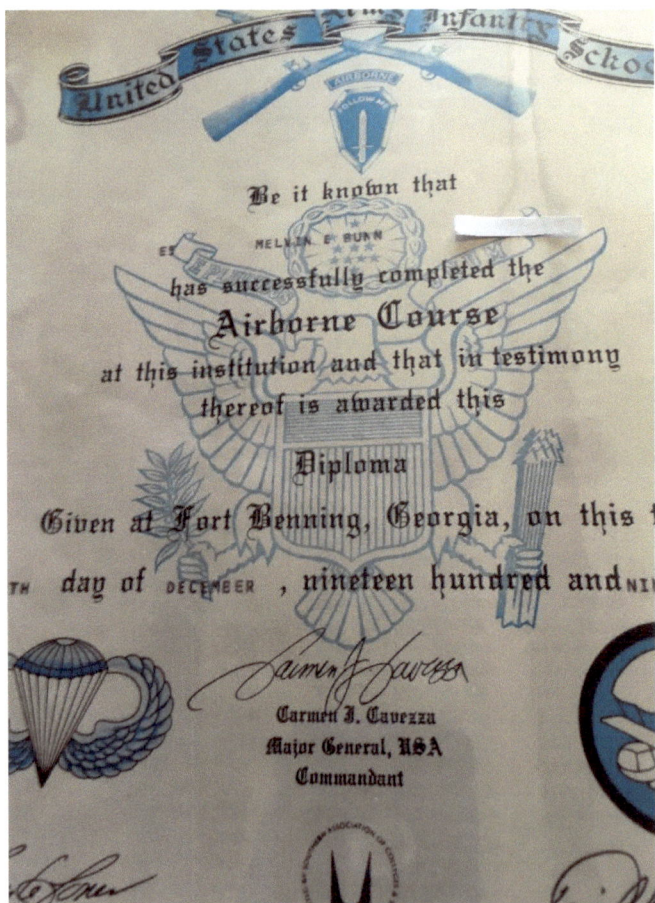

United States Army Infantry School

Be it known that

MELVIN E. BURN

has successfully completed the

Airborne Course

at this institution and that in testimony
thereof is awarded this

Diploma

Given at Fort Benning, Georgia, on this
day of DECEMBER , nineteen hundred and NI

Carmen J. Cavezza
Major General, USA
Commandant

LIFE AFTER THE MILITARY SUMARRY

It was rare to see any black combat engineers that were airborne rangers throughout my career, I only knew of one in my field and he was a Ranger but did not have his Airborne Wings.

I was hot, so I did everything in my power to stay there but since I had never been overseas, I had to move with the group. At least that is what I was told.

I had a lot of things going on, I was getting ready to have my first baby in May, I was purchasing a house and having my household items shipped a typical move with the regular stresses.

I just was going to bide my time until I got out the service.

The Ranger tab was something I had earned and no one could take it away from me.

The war motivated me to get back engaged into being a dedicated soldier.

I took the oath of reenlistment on the 29th of October 1990. I decided that I was going to do one more tour and get out. The main reason I decided to do the tour is because I was guaranteed being able to pcs to Fort Sill. The second reason is because they were not letting no one out the service at that time they were just extending the time because of the war. I finally received orders to pcs to Fort Sill in December of 1991. I took 30 days leave and was supposed to report to my new unit in February around the first week. My intentions were to do my 4 years at Fort Sill and get out but when I reached Fort Sill, the unit I was assigned to, the entire brigade was moving to Fort Carson, Colorado.

I had to make a hard decision to leave my newborn and wife at Fort Sill with my mother and Bishop Truitt.

After I was forced to move to Fort Carson Colorado, I was literally cold, bitter and just wanted to do the rest of my obligated service time and make a quick and quiet exit out the military.

Honorable Discharge

from the Armed Forces of the United States of America

This is to certify that

MELVIN EUGENE BUNN   SGT   USAR

was Honorably Discharged from the

United States Army

on the 22ND *day of* NOVEMBER 1994 *This certificate is awarded as a*
testimonial of Honest and Faithful Service

Looking back now, I probably could have stuck it out and did a couple of more tours but it all worked out for the good.

I went back to school and used my GI bill for my first year out and then I started working for the Federal Aviation Administration (FAA).

Most of the private sector and the government sector was all about politics, not necessarily what you knew but who you knew and how they could help you advance from one position to the other, FAA was no different.

They were mandated to hire so many veterans and the culture had to be diverse, it was supposed to reflect the community in which one lived.

As a civilian, one thing I had to get use to was people in general do not take you at your word. It was almost like anything you said was on hold until it was proven.

I would tell people that I was an airborne Ranger and the look on their face said I was lying, like no way could this guy be a Ranger.

One of my co-workers that still had military connections even went to the point to call his buddy that was still serving and looked at my c--file and my dd-214 to see if I was telling the truth. The reason why I know he gained access to my c-file was because my co-worker could only know the information through my c-file because a lot of the information was deemed need to know material. It also included my evaluations from the Ranger Course that he quoted what the instructor had told me in school.

Even though he had gotten the information illegally, from that time forward he had another level of respect for me.

Being questioned over the years, even today when I wear my Ranger paraphernalia the main question I get asked is, were you really a Ranger and the second question I get is how many jumps you have made. I sometimes want to be facetious and say something smart like, how many jumps do you have? But I usually direct them to an interview that I did a couple of years back on the OMA radio station where I was interviewed as an Airborne Ranger or I tell them to put my name in YouTube and the interview will come up.

Deborah and I have been blessed to have a total of three children, 2 girls and 1 son.

My oldest one is a proud graduate of OU, my baby girl is a proud graduate of UCO and my boy will soon be a proud graduate of OSU.

I am retired and finally getting the chance to relax and write my books and tell my stories. I always wanted to write several books and decided that I would complete at least 3 of the 5 books I said that I would write. Night Ranger is the first book of mine to come out in 2021, my goal is to release a different book every 3 months this year if the good Lord keeps me around. None of us know when our time is up that is why I believe in living life to the fullest because tomorrow is not guaranteed.

.

THIS PAGE INTENTIONALLY LEFT BLANK

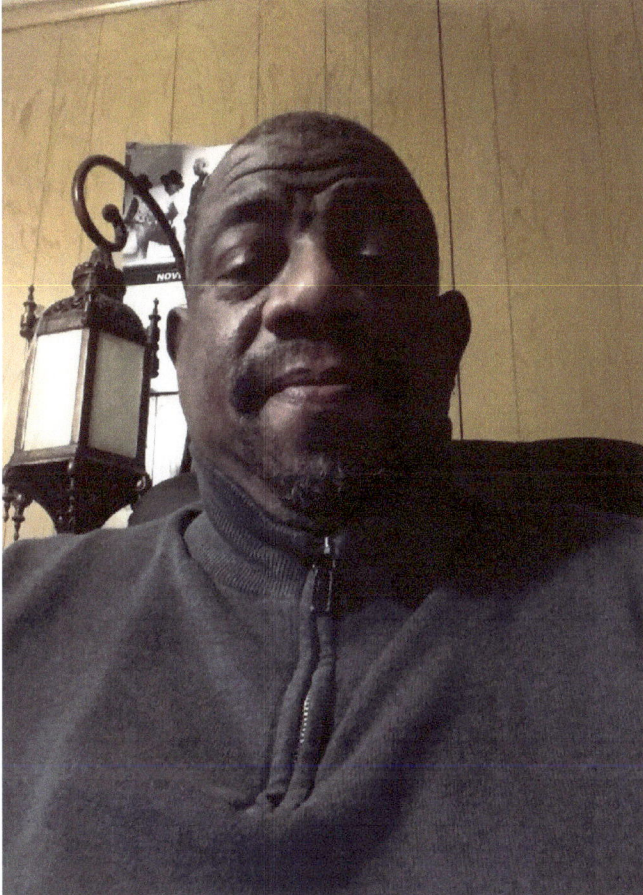

SUMMARY

This book gives the reader a snapshot of my life in the military, many people served in the different services but few are fortunate enough to say that they were an airborne Ranger.

I am and will always be proud of the fact that I was able to experience such a feat. I share some of the challenges I experienced, some highs and lows and some of my accomplishments along the way. I have been out the military now for over 26 years so I was only able to recall just a fraction of the situations that I experienced and went through. I hope the reader finds humor, joy, a scene of pride from my story.

Public Service Announcement (PSA)#4

It is fitting that I finish writing my first book on inauguration day January 20,2021. As the day represent a new start and a new beginning this book also will be the start of new beginnings for my 1ˢᵗ of many books. We celebrate our 46 President of the United States of America Joe Biden and vice President Kamala Harris as they assume their leadership positions. Which bring me to my last public service announcement in this book. It is important that each and every one of us register

to vote and vote in the state and local elections.
It is imperative that you allow your voice to be
heard.

The song writer was right, old soldiers never
die; they just fade away.

Rangers Lead The Way!

Keep up with Ranger Bunn

bunnsworld.com
BUNN'S
WORLD
A PLACE TO RELAX AND FIND
TOOLS THAT WILL HELP YOU
BECOME BETTER AND DO BETTER
TOWARDS MANKIND
Get Support
G POSTS

My website

Melvin E. Bunn
6 subscribers

EDIT CHANNEL   MANAGE VIDEOS

Uploads

2:08

My YouTube Channel

MEL SR MUSIC

Check out my music! Discover us on Shazam. Download the album from Apple iTunes, Google Play Music, Amazon Music, 7 Digital, and 24-7. Stream on Spotify, Apple Music, Tidal, Deezer, Anghami, and Napster. Click the links below for song samples. Lyric Videos coming soon to YouTube!

Melvin E. Bunn
Smooth Dog

Get Support

NIGHT RANGER

BY

MELVIN E BUNN

Order your copy of our first book
TODAY!

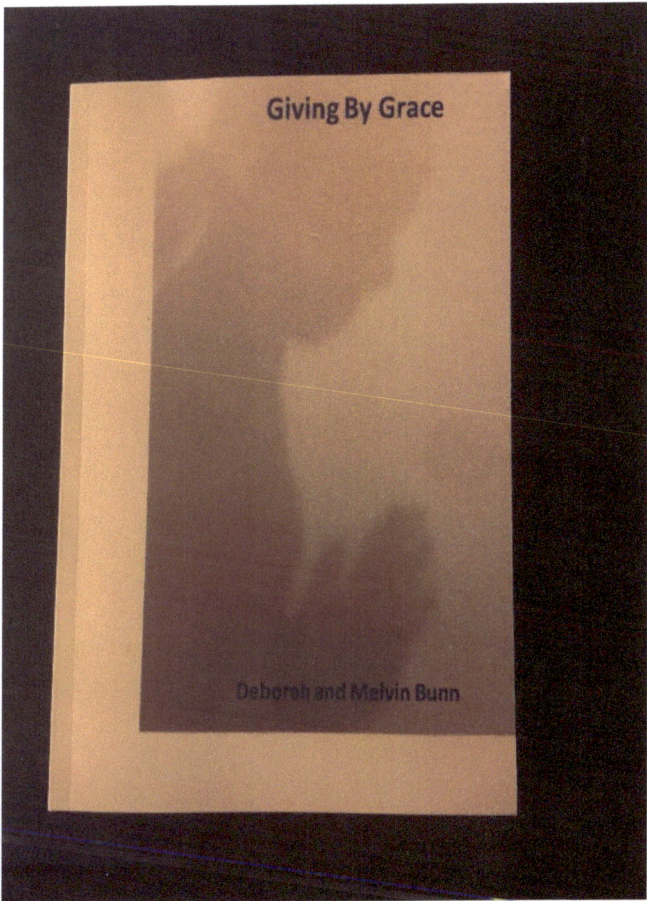

Giving By Grace

Deborah and Melvin Bunn

www.amazon.com/books

NIGHT RANGER

ABOUT THIS BOOK

This book was wrote based off of my life experience as an airborne ranger in the United States Army. It gives my account as I remembered it. I have been out the military for over 26 years now so my memory is not as sharp as it was back then but it gives the reader the picture of some of the challenges going through the Ranger Course and some of the issues that I faced.

MELVIN E. BUNN

I am a proud resident of Oklahoma City, OK
I want to say thank you to each person, who has invested in me and my success. I hope this book brings the reader joy, humor and a sense of pride from my story. Until next time.

RANGERS LEAD THE WAY!